Why YELLOW Matters

And 30 other thoughts to make your things matter more.
Lyle Smith.

Book & cover design by Rocket.
ISBN 979-8-9892659-0-9

Dedication

For ever challenging. For ever encouraging. For ever patient. For ever, Heather. For ever inspiring. For ever curious. For ever appreciating it all. For ever, Aiden.

A Note from the Author

You may notice what you may think are a few unusual spellings and terminology included here.

Like "hed" and "subhed" for "head" and "subhead," or "TK" for "to come."

These are intentional.

They come from the old newspaper tradition.

I learned them in my earliest days of professional writing and editing.

I couldn't change these habits now if I tried.

Or wanted to.

Enjoy them for what they are and please don't let them distract you.

If I knew where they came from, I would tell you.

I just know that this is the way they've always been done. Far be it from me to insist on a change now.

11   If you read nothing else in this book. Read **This.**

This.

I didn't set out to write a book. I just had one idea one day that I thought was important and I started writing it down.

One thought about how to do things. Better.

How I do things when I do them well.

And I thought it might be valuable to others.
And it made me think up a few other ideas. Better ideas.

Things I hadn't noticed anyone else noticing.

Because that's how ideas work. Sometimes.

How good ideas work. Most of the time.

One after another after another.

I started writing about those things that matter to me.
Writing. Communicating. Uncovering a few of those things some people think they're protecting others from knowing.

Things that I think should matter to other people.

That more than sometimes matter to other people.

And I just kept going.

And I realized a common thread.

The things we believe.

Or misbelieve.

The things we think we understand.

Or those things we thought we understood.

That we did not.

Not really.

Because maybe we don't take the time to think about them.

And maybe I'm wrong.

But at least I'm making you think them through. Again.

###

I don't presume that what I think will change your world.

But I think it might.

Once upon a time, someone thought something up. And someone else read it. And absorbed it. And took it to do what he or she thought would matter in the world.

And made a story of their own.

And that is what all of this is all about.

Believe things.

That's the most important thing.

Then question them.

Then understand you misbelieved them.

Then take them to the next place.

And make that place better than the last place.

And leave it better.

Part One
THINKING THINGS

Part One / Thinking Things

Why Yellow Matters

I don't know why. I just like it.

I know it's better.

Faster.

Lighter.

It makes me run faster, jump higher, play better.

It's waaaay cooler.

I'll get compliments.

It'll get me noticed.

I just know.

We spend tons of time and boatloads of money doing research and analysis of every bit of data we can lay our hands on trying to understand why people choose things.

To understand what makes them buy one thing over another.

To predict how our product should be designed.

How our service is perceived.

We try to automate it.

We try to game the search engine.

We try to slip something in under the door.

We toss it pell-mell over the transom.

Just to get it in front of the eyeballs that matter. The eyeballs belonging to the people we think matter. That matter most to us.

But how do we know?

We gather all the evidence and try our best to cull an understanding of… what? Behavior? Preference? Decision-making?

And sometimes it helps. A little. Sometimes a bunch.

But in the end… people are people. And they choose based on what matters to them. Inside their own noggin.

There's an old story that Coca Cola didn't sell… at all… I mean people wouldn't even try it… until they put caramel color into it and turned it from its unnatural and weird green to the dark, syrupy, Coke color we all know and love today.

I don't know if there's truth to that story. But it rings true.

I have two pairs of running shoes. They are both exactly the same. One pair is blue. The other is yellow. Same mileage. Same amount of wear. Same size. Same fit. Exactly the same.
Even with my eyes closed.

And I'll spend an extra 15 minutes searching for the other yellow one instead of just lacing up the easy-to-find blue pair because I know, deeply, innately, desperately, that they are better.

It's irrational.

I'm irrational. We all are.

I know it. You know it.

And I live with it. The same way we all do.

Every day.

And the only way anyone else can know why yellow matters is to pay attention.

Why Surprises Matter

It happens to the best of us.

That nagging feeling. Something you had really, really high hopes for just doesn't seem like it's panning out.

It feels uphill.

It feels heavy.

It feels like it should be crumpled up and tossed in the bin.
And set on fire. Or set out to sea. Or buried in concrete.

It is disappointing.

So you let it sit.

You're literally frightened at what you'll think of it if you open that file to read it or listen to it again.

But you know you have to.

It's the thing we all think about from time to time, but never say out loud.

"Yeah… that's not my best work."

You never want to be saying that to yourself when you're the one delivering the work.

And…

You really never want to be the one thinking that when you're the one receiving the work.

###

I landed a dream guest for my podcast recently. I couldn't wait.
I prepared. I wrote up a whole journey of questions. I was so excited to get it I couldn't contain myself.

Then, during the recording, I was sure I'd made a mistake.

I was absolutely sure I'd botched it up. But good.

So I didn't listen to it right away.

I let it sit.

And sit.

And sit.

I moved on to other things.

Some good. Some great. Some just adequate.

But that thing was just sitting. Talking to me from the back of my mind. Reminding me it was still there. Daring me to listen to it. Staking a claim that I shouldn't just junk it wholesale.

I tried to listen to it. Several times. I started, then stopped. Just couldn't get myself amped up enough to drive back the fear and do it.

Then, one day, I was running out of new material. I had to get something out. So, I decided I needed to take my medicine. And I started listening.

And the most remarkable thing happened.

It was actually pretty good.

No… it was better than pretty good.

In the end, it may be the best one I've ever done.

And I'm kicking myself for delaying the work so long.

And I'm surprised. Deeply surprised.

And that's a feeling I'm going to have to make a point of remembering.

Often, the things that feel less than at first ...

... may just be hiding something important.

In a moment, that defeated, dejected feeling can give way to the energy of inspired momentum.

Don't ever be afraid of the surprises you may find in your own work.

Why Time Matters

Epiphany
/ə'pifənə'

a moment of sudden revelation or insight.
Middle English: from Greek epiphainein 'reveal.'

###

I came to one recently.

That is ... speed is not all it's cracked up to be.

Absolutely, time is a valuable resource not to be wasted.

But that doesn't always mean you need to get things done faster at all costs.
All it really means is - don't WASTE it.

It takes time to get things done right.

And right is the key.

Stop rushing things out the door just for the sake of rushing them out the door.

It's important to get them ready for prime time before you send them on their way.

As a former newsman, I was trained in the culture of deadlines. To be a creature of the clock.

We celebrated speed.

Get it done fast and get it out to the people who need it... to read it. Today - every day. This week - every week.

It is a habit that's discouragingly hard to break.

No doubt deadlines are important.

But the flip-side of that gold doubloon is something else... quality... utility... usefulness.

Is that thing you got out there into the world helping someone? Valuable to someone?

Not pursuit of perfection, mind you. Though perfection is a fine thing to find. It's about taking the time to get it right.

To make it mean something. To someone else.

So take the time to get it right.

But not so much that it gets in the way of your progress.

It's a balance.

What's the epiphany?

It's not that time doesn't matter. It's not that speed isn't important.

Just not as important as it may seem.

I can trace almost every big mistake I've ever made to speed.
More specifically… rushing. Intended with all good intention,
but in the end, rushing was at the center of the mistake.
The bad decision.

They say when you're a hammer, every problem looks like a nail. Well, when
you're a creature of the clock… a runner… a racer…
every solution starts to look like speed.

Hours per person. Billable hours. Even sometimes just looking busy.
All the time.

Speed is a great asset. Use it where you can. Use it where it makes sense.
But don't let it get in the way of your strategy. Distract you from your goal.

Take the time to get it right.

Why Perspective Matters

It ain't about you, Sport.

So much communication is built on the idea that you have something you want someone else to understand.

Or know.

Or engage with.

The problem is those people don't think about you that way.

At all.

Ever.

They think about what they have. Or sometimes what they haven't.

What they want.

What they need.

To succeed.

To advance.

To grow and thrive.

So that ultra important thing you want to communicate to them…

… most of the time…

Matters more to you than it does to them.

So you have a vested interest…

… among all of your other vested interests…

To think through their eyes.

To walk in their shoes.

To see their world the way they see it.

Just so you can communicate that ultra important thing of yours to them in a way that fits the puzzle space they are so desperately trying to fill.

They have to see you as their missing piece.

Specifically.

Related to what they have and have not.

To what they want.

To what they need.

So the thing you're connected to is the same thing that will help them to succeed.

To advance.

To grow and thrive.

So they understand it is the thing that will make their lives better, stronger, faster.

Easier.

It's not about you.

Or your thing.

It never was.

Part One / Thinking Things

Why 'The Zone' Matters

We all do things for a reason.

You know it.

You don't walk under a ladder.

You don't step on a crack in the sidewalk.

You don't break a mirror.

Spill salt. Toss a pinch over your left shoulder.

Never, ever leave a hat on a bed.

Baseball pitchers jump over the foul lines to ward off bad luck. Players wear "rally caps," refuse to shave, walk the same direction out their front doors to preserve a streak. When a pitcher has a shutout, no-hitter, or perfect game going, the pitcher sits alone on the bench.

Serena Williams wore the same winning socks every match.

Michael Jordan wore his UNC practice shorts under his Bulls uniform every game.

Tiger Woods always wears red on Sunday. Lee Trevino wore a red shirt AND socks before him.

When I play golf, I always pull my coin from my left-hand pocket and place it tails up with my right hand to mark my spot on the green. And I always carry at least three tees in my right-hand pocket. If I break one, I need to pull another from my bag before hitting another shot.

Why?

I don't know.

I don't remember when I started it.

But I'm sure it helps me.

In the theater, it is bad luck to offer "good luck." Instead, say "break a leg."

They won't say Macbeth, either. It must be "the Scottish play." And if they say it, they must walk 'round outside the theater building, turn around three times and spit in order to reverse the curse.

And never, ever whistle. You'll jinx us all.

There are real reasons for all of these real things we do. Real history and real events and real people that real things happened to, forever linked to these habits and fears.

In the 1999 baseball film "For the Love of the Game," aging pitcher Billy Chapel eyes up the Yankees fans shouting their words of love and encouragement to him in that unique Bronx way.

Inside his head, he says simply "clear the mechanism," and all the sound stops. The focus of his vision shifts and all he sees is the batter, the catcher, and his own task at hand.

Is it superstition?

Is it silly?

Is it sometimes, maybe most times, ridiculous?

Yes.

But do we stop doing it?

No.

When I use a pen, I write with the same pen I picked up for myself on a trip in 2001.

I use different types of notebooks for different types of work. Every time.

I hit return six times at the top of a blank page before I start writing. Anything.

I'll bet you have at least one of these habits, too. And I'll bet that when you skip it, or ignore it, things don't seem to go as smoothly as you expected. And you wonder where the magic went.

Good luck things drive bad luck things away.

And it is not about luck. At all.

It's about the zone.

The flow.

Feeling right in the moment.

It's ritual. To put us in mind of doing great things.

Part One / Thinking Things

Why Quiet Chaos Matters

Where'd he go?

It happened often.

Not every day, but almost every day.

There were a whole lot of things he did - and didn't do -
as a leader that I didn't like - or agree with all the time.

But he was the best creative director I ever had for a few other
fundamental reasons.

His office was big.

And on a corner.

Overlooking Third Avenue.

And a mess.

A godawful mess.

But a good mess.

A welcoming, comfortable mess.

Piles and piles of magazines and newspapers and envelopes all over the place. Subscriptions that didn't make sense. Didn't match what we were doing. Or his interests. Or anything he might ever want to read.

But that's not why they were there.

It took me a couple of rounds of it to understand. But eventually it became clear.

We'd have another kickoff meeting.

A new client.

An established client.

Whatever it might be, it was a new assignment.

We'd get our marching orders to go keep making progress on the work we had in the pipeline.

And he'd disappear.

He'd close his door.

He'd let us knock to ask a question if we needed him, but it was clear we shouldn't unless it was absolutely necessary.

Unless there was something on deadline that would inevitably be missed to make something more perfect.

This was his relationship with the value of time - especially at the end of the day.

This was one of the things I didn't agree with mentioned at the top. And a story for another time.

This other thing. This disappearing thing. This was new to me.
A different approach.

No team brainstorming, although we did that, too, from time to time.
Ineffectively.

This was a deep dive. Solo. A free-dive.
A creative meditation.

Time undistracted.

Page after page. Skipped. Ruffled. Torn. Folded. Crumpled.

Twain said the difference between amateurs and professionals was that
amateurs borrow, while professionals just steal, outright.

The thinking. The images. The words. The ideas that always came when
the door opened again.

Borrowed or stolen, then massaged to make something new.
Something different. Something right for the message.

There's no such thing as writer's block when you take the time
in the quiet to let it come.

Then we gathered. To get our direction.

Then we collaborated. To make it all better.

Brainstorming is a phantom where I come from.

We try it, because everyone thinks it's a generator. An idea engine.

But, it's the independent thinking that generates the seed.
From which great things grow.

Why Next Steps Matter

Nothing is possible.

Or impossible.

There is always a solution of some kind.

A next step.

It might not be the one you were thinking about
when you got started.

It might not seem achievable from the seat you occupy
in the moment.

But there is always a way from where you are toward where you
want to be. Or where you need to be.

Change your perspective.

Take your time.

Think differently.

Never confuse movement with action.

Or stillness with lack of progress.

The next step may not be forward.

The path to where you're headed almost never looks like a straight line.

Avoid. Challenge. Overcome.

Achieve. Dodge. Leap.

All to get past the places and things and people who play minor roles in your story.

Where you are in the moment may seem dire.

The mountain in front of you may seem insurmountable.

The distance you need to go may seem unthinkable.

But there is a way.

There's always a way.

Think.

Prepare.

Solve.

Repeat.

Give me four hours to fell a tree and I'll spend the first three and a half sharpening the axe.

Be your best when things are at their worst.

The path will present itself.

Nothing is possible.

Or impossible.

The next step always belongs to you.

Part One / Thinking Things

Why That Moment Matters

I was early.

Where I was going wasn't open yet.

And I found myself without tools. No computer. No tablet. No notebook.
No pen or pencil. And I was irritated at the prospect of wasting the time.

A new friend wrote down recently that he believed there was no problem
so big that it couldn't be explained on an A4 sheet of paper.
That's 8.5 x 11 for us on this side of the Atlantic.

There was a store right there. And a coffee place. So I bought a pad of paper
and a pen and all of a sudden, I had everything I needed to get everything
I wanted to do done.

For those of you finding yourself in a similar predicament.
For those not in the same profession as I ...

I'm not a writer, you say.
But it's not true, says I.

Not true at all.

Ok, it's partly true, like most things. And we can discuss the art and craft of
writing as a marketable skill another time.

But stripped down to essentials, writing is something we all do. All the time.

Whether you recognize it or not. Whether you believe it or not. Whether you write it down or not.

Writing is the act of creating.

The Beatles didn't read or write music. Did they still "write" songs?

The lyrics written down in notebooks. The chord changes, too. And then recorded. For sound. For us.

Writing is thinking made physical.

We write notes. Doodles. Scribbles. They all have value. Often more than we recognize at the time.

Whether you're leaving a note for someone, capturing something to remember later, or just trying to figure something out.

The most important writing isn't about the scrolls and books and libraries. The databases. The most important writing comes in much smaller pieces.

We look at our grand repositories of information and learning as the most valuable products.

We think of these places as safe and secure today, but remember the great library at Alexandria was burned down.

And the dark ages descended upon Europe.

And then... we started to write things down anew.

Technology, as we think about it today, is so good. So wonderful for so many different reasons. So many tools to make things easier. To do more.

To give us access to more.

But sometimes we forget.

... that every great thing produced in the world began with a note scribbled on a scrap of paper.

Or an envelope.

Or a napkin.

A doodle.

A fragment.

A diagram.

As children, we learned one of the original technologies after fire ... and the wheel ... was paper. Papyrus. The Egyptian thing that would become paper.

But why?

So we could write it all down and take it with us.

What happened, when, and where.

How we did things. What's going on now. What comes next.

Writing is thinking made physical. And portable.

It is understanding spread wide.

And it doesn't take any new tools or technology at all.

All it takes is time. And enough quiet to think. And write it down.
So you can share it with other people.

I was early.

And I was afraid it was going to be time wasted.

But I had a pen and paper.

And it was the most valuable moment in my day.

Why Specificity Matters

It is the most important thing.

Why?

We want to appeal to the largest number possible. Build a big audience. A following. A vast customer base.

So why not try to speak to everyone?

We believe what we do, what we make, is good for everyone.

So we try to speak. To everyone.

We're changing the world.

So we speak to the whole world. All at once. We cast a wide net. We open up all channels. We shout from the rooftops. And who cares?

Simply... who? cares?

Appealing to everyone appeals to no one.

Counterintuitive? No. It's true.

Who? Cares? That's who needs to hear from you.

All of your power is in the specific.

The catalyst that drives the reaction.

What do you mean to that man? That woman? That child?
That business?

How does what you make or do make them live better?

Connect the dots.

Specifically.

Appealing to everyone appeals to no one.

Appealing to one can achieve universality.

Stop speaking to everybody.

Stop casting your net wide.

Drop a line.

Be specific.

Trust that the audience who understands is out there. They are.
Connect with him. With her. With them.

They'll find you if you speak to them. Directly.

You want a large following? Speak to one.

It is the thing that makes you … effective. It's where the power lies.

The definition tells you what you need to know.

###
spe-se-əfi-sə-tē
noun: the quality or condition of being specific: such as
a) the condition of being peculiar to a particular individual or group of organisms
b) the condition of participating in or catalyzing only one or a few chemical reactions

###

In Biology, it is the narrowness of the range of substances with which an antibody or other agent acts or is EFFECTIVE.

Get outside the range and the reaction doesn't happen.

General doesn't mean anything.

Specificity is everything. The most important thing.

Why?

Because. That's why.

Part One / Thinking Things

Why The Front Gate Matters

Who do you have standing at the gate?

Content matters.

Always has.

And in more ways than one.

And quality, too.

Theories and methods and methodologies abound.

Post early and often.

Keywords. Long-tail. White hat / black hat. Feed the engines.

But what happens when they get there?

Your quality makes the machines hum, but what about the people?

How do they respond when they find you?

What does your content say to them?

Does it answer the question they were asking when they were looking for you?

When they found you?

Does it cast them as a character in your story?

Or better, cast you as a character in their story?

Who's in charge of making sure it does?

Who's in charge of making sure your message means something?

To them?

To anyone?

There's a quality equation there, too.

Human quality.

And there's a gap between the machines and the humans.

And you need someone to make sure your message has discipline.

Some say publish every day and you'll never worry about revenue again.

But what are you publishing?

And who's guarding the gates for you?

Part Two
DECIDING THINGS

Part Two / Deciding Things

Why Simple Matters

Never confuse simple with easy.

Ever.

They are not the same.

Never the same.

Even if so many want to force them into the same box of synonyms.

Simple is beautiful in its uncomplicated, understandable nature.

Easy is easy.

Simple is about writing. And thinking. And being seen for the value it brings. Simple is about inspiration.

Easy is a choice. Only about execution.

Simple is the better description of the complex. The communication they all understand. The actionable of the options. The obvious of the choices.

Easy is easy.

Simple is attractive. It makes you want to make a choice.
It leads you down the path to something that matters.
Something significant. Simple that makes you realize things.

Easy is easy.

Simple takes time to plot out. To understand and communicate to others.
Simple is strategic and specific. Sometimes startlingly so.
Sometimes blindingly so.

Easy is easy.

Simple requires time. Requires effort. Requires thought and analysis.
Sometimes or often consultation and teamwork. Simple can change things.
Simple can lead you to epiphanies. Simple is an invitation to aspiration.

Easy is easy.

At its most valuable, simple is more challenging than most care to admit.

Never confuse SIMPLE with EASY.

Why Ideas Matter

Some ideas seem to change the world all on their own.

And some ideas seem great, but never get off the ground.

The truth is ideas fail. Sometimes. More than sometimes. Ideas fail all the time.

Even great ones.

That's the reality of our world.

Great ideas fail sometimes. And bad ideas sometimes succeed.

But why?

Did it fail because it was a bad idea?

Did it fail somewhere between idea and execution?

Did it fail because the people didn't like it?

Or did it fail because the people just didn't understand it?

Great ideas can make you see into the future.

Great ideas are exciting, and energizing, and motivating, and inspiring. To you.

But what are ideas to other people?

More often than not, the reason people don't gravitate toward something is because they can't see how it matters. TO THEM.

They don't understand it.

What it is. What it does. Why it is important. TO THEM.

And that's unforgivable.

A great idea, poorly explained, cannot survive.

The time spent working to clearly communicate the idea that means everything to you and why it should mean everything TO THEM is just as important as any time you spend developing that idea.

Maybe more.

If you can't clearly communicate...

What it is. Who it's for.

Why it's valuable to that other human being.

You're digging yourself into a hole.

They can't see it if you can't show them.

Take the time to get the story of your idea straight.

Because a great idea, poorly explained, cannot survive.

Why Guides Matter

You can get good help these days. You just have to know where to look for it.

What do you need? We can do that!

But can they, really?

Maybe they can. Maybe not.

It takes understanding on both sides to get to the answer.

Maybe they're getting ahead of themselves.

Maybe they're not asking the right questions at all.

And you may not be giving the right answers.

What do you need?

If the answer is a thing. A website. An email campaign. A funnel.
A brochure. An annual report. You're probably going to be disappointed.

In the end.

They may be able to do it.

They may be able to do it well, even.

But they're just taking an order.

One from column A. One from column B.

What do you need?

If the answer is what that thing does. A result.

That's a different question entirely. One that requires a different answer.

Grow your business. Improve your reputation. Generate more qualified leads. Get more people to know you. Get you from the consideration set to over the hump.

The conversation REQUIRES more questions and more answers. Many more. And going deep.

To define the value. To define your story. To figure out how best to share your story. And where. And with whom. And why.

Simple questions beget simple answers.

Bigger aspiration requires bigger thinking and bigger stories.

So many creatives, consultants, agencies out there are order-takers.

Too many.

They rely on you to do all the work. All the planning. All the thinking.

They rely on you to be the expert.

They translate expert in your business or industry to expert in everything.

Then they take your order and execute on that alone.

They're not your partner.

They're not your guide.

They're not really experts at all.

They may tell you so.

But if they're not challenging you, they're not who they may claim to be.

They may get the job done. But it may not be what you had in mind.

It's like pulling out a hammer to unstick a window.

Or using a chainsaw to slice your baguette.

Or a stick of dynamite to rid your garden of a ground hog.

It'll work in a pinch, but it's not really the right choice.

It's not the thing that will help you get to where you're going. Not really.

There are guides and there are order-takers.

There is no in between.

Guides know the way down the path.

And they can help you along your journey to where you want to go.

Order-takers see themselves as a tool and look to you for the solution.

Listen to the questions.

Understand your answers inspire the solution.

That's where you'll see the difference.

Why Your Team Matters

Who is the most dangerous player on the field?

Because it's not the best player. Not always.

The most dangerous player is the one who raises his or her game to meet the moment.

The runner who's readiest at the right time for the right race.

The golfer who peaks for the Major.

The hitter who sees the right pitch at the right time and gets on base.

The big-game, post-season, late-game athlete who gets graced with a nickname like Captain Clutch, Magic, the Chairman of the Boards. Grasping victory from the jaws of defeat. "Bucky f***ing Dent!"

What makes this competitor most dangerous?

The kids on the playground always pick the kid who loves to win first.

Sure. That's the fun kid. The kid who likes to celebrate. The kid who attracts all the other fun playground kids.

But what about the kid who hates to lose? The one with attitude. The one with the face. You know the one.

No matter what happens in the game, race, or competition, the player who hates to lose will do anything, everything to find a way to pull it out.

Not playing, running, jumping, or throwing her or his best that day? Adjust, improvise, and find a way to get the most out of the moment.

The player who loves to win struggles with coming from behind. Struggles with adversity and things outside his or her control. Outcome only.

In an unbalanced match, this is exactly who you need. The shock and awe. Zero sum. Without victory, what's the purpose?

When it's toe-to-toe, tough-as-nails, face-to-face… not so much.

Suffer a blow? It's a shock to the system.

Bought into your own press? Can't see a way through to the final buzzer, bell, or breaking of the tape.

When you hate to lose, you see the game differently.

It's a living thing. It ebbs and flows. And you test them with every effort. Victory is important, but only part of the game.

There are small victories every step of the way. Even in a loss, you notch wins against your own abilities.

Great racehorses are described as being "game."
It means they just like to race.

It's what drives the best of us to succeed in life. To recognize growth in failure. Victory in compromise. Nobility in pushing the pendulum back the other direction.

It is how we bring out the best in each other.

It's how we should always choose our teams.

Part Two / Deciding Things

Why Clever Matters

By half.

It's an ironic Britishism.

Meaning a half more than full. Or half again as much.
Or just too much!

Add the clever and it means too smart for one's own good.

Clever is the enemy of the clear.

Clever can feel like a great asset.

We all like to be seen as clever.

Clever can make you feel like the smartest person in the room.

Make you feel like you're rising above.

Guiding. Teaching. Leading.

On the other hand…

All the other people in that room can get cheesed off when you use it with too much, what?

Flair? Panache? Gusto?

It can be underhanded.

You become arrogant.

No one likes to feel less than.

Ah hah! is motivational.

Clarity. Clouds parting. Epiphany is what makes Ah hah! work.

Beware the clever turn of phrase.

When you write your brand language.

Your strap line. Your tag lines. Your calls to action.

Be clear.

Clever is the enemy of the clear.

It's you speaking to yourself.

When you need to speak to THEM.

It's you entertaining yourself.

When you need to be delivering for THEM.

What do I know that they do not know?

They don't care.

They want to know, what's in it for me?

What does all this mean to me?

How does this thing make me, my life, better for me?

In order to be heard. The message must be clear and compelling.

If not.

Who cares?

No one.

Clever requires unpacking.

Specific frame of reference.

A decoder ring.

You've seen them. Those lines that mean nothing. Those ads that must mean something to someone, but not you. Those speeches clearly about something important, but you can't, for the life of you, figure out what?

Be clever.

For yourself.

Lock the inside jokes inside.

Inside is where it's safe to be too clever by half.

That's where they can call you on it. And you'll appreciate it.
Learn from it.

Outside is different.

Smart is an asset. Smart is important. But smart for its own audience
can be too much. Sometimes.

Be clear. Be concise. Be heard.

Why Balance Matters

Yes. It does some amazing things.

All you have to do is ask the right questions.

And it seems like magic.

But it's not.

People have worried about artificial intelligence since, well, since they developed their own natural intelligence. And imagination.

I've worried about AI since at least the summer of 1984 when a soldier was sent back in time to defeat the machines.

When my buddies and I sat in a multiplex in Morristown, NJ, four nights in a row watching The Terminator.

When AI ran amok.

It wasn't magic. It was dangerous. And destructive. And terrifying. And thrilling.

And you have to wonder why is it that whenever we think about something escaping our control it takes the form of a malign threat to humanity?

It's never a tool that makes the world a better place.

When the machines take over in the story, it's amazing and unsettling. It seems supernatural. But it's not magic.

Because magic is just a perspective on what you're seeing. It's what we want to see.

The beauty in magic is in the trick. We all want to believe it. We all want to believe it's possible. We know it's not, but we are all delighted and amazed when we see it happen before our own eyes.

But that doesn't make it real.

It's a game.

It's a trick.

It's an illusion.

It's a tool.

That, in the best of hands, can make the world work a bit easier for us all.

In the best of hands.

The AI we're seeing now is only as good as the input it gets.

People have considered for generations that computers can only be as smart and savvy as the people who program them.

At least for now.

Garbage in, garbage out.

When you prompt the tools with clear, logical expectations, they deliver a better result.

When you leave out the details, it delivers something less. And exactly what you should expect.

It can't read your mind.

But it can learn. Sort-of.

I've tried using some of these tools in my own life and business. AI has existed for years in smaller forms. But this is new. And different. And, surprise, as I get better at using the tools, they get more helpful to me.

They speed things up.

Make things a bit easier.

Allow me to concentrate on the bigger ideas.

Sort of exactly what every tool ever invented was, basically, designed to do.

Make our lives easier.

If we continue to think of new developments in technology as tools, the way we always have, rather than as magical saviors, or worse, as threats to our very existence, the picture comes into better focus.

But on the other hand, we should take heed of the people in the know who are warning caution to the world as well.

Balance is important in all things.

Take the time to understand the impact of what we are trying to accomplish.

And don't rush things.

A recurring theme here.

Take the time to get it right.

It is important.

Because remember, time always marches on and the post-apocalyptic world of The Terminator was only set in 2029.

And if we've learned anything from the glory that is science fiction,
it's that when we give up the controls, we give up control.

Why Vision Matters

So many present themselves as experts.

Yet some speak about the thing in which they are supposedly expert in exactly the wrong way.

Their puzzle has missing pieces.

Or they only talk about some of the pieces, forgetting the bigger picture.

Where are we headed?

Why?

What path is the right path for us? Our team? Our customers?

Strategy.

It occupies a very specific spot in the marketing communications food chain.

The brand's story feeds into the brand's strategy.

The tactics you select support the strategy.

And it's all perched atop your revolutionary product, your stellar and unique service, the delivery method you use to delight your customers and change the world.

Yet so often, they get pulled into the gravitational pull of a preferred tactic. A happy talent. Without establishing or even acknowledging the strategy.

Strategy without tactics is the slowest route to victory, says Sun Tzu.

Vision versus action.

Innovation verus execution.

You need to have both. To be excellent.

You need to give your time to the first in order to know which of the second will serve you.

It's bigger than some realize.

But they aren't afraid to tell you they're experts.   .

Ask them about the strategy.

See if it makes sense. Holds up. Passes the logic test.

Then decide for yourself who the expert is.

Because Sun Tzu also said tactics without strategy is the noise before defeat.

And that is not the music you wish to hear.

Why The Right Things Matter

It isn't everything. It's the only thing.

You don't win because you're better.

The better player loses all the time.

The better athlete finishes second all the time. Or third. Or fourth. Or worse.

Better talent. Better skills. Better speed. Better agility.

In the moment, better means nothing.

You set records because you're better.

You set records because you're faster, stronger, have better eyesight. You're calmer when you pull the trigger or loose the arrow. You have a better left leg. Right leg. You can throw 100 miles an hour. You set records sometimes because you train better. You can run more miles. And not get injured. Throw more pitches. Spend more time on the field or in the gym. You have better genes. You're faster-twitch. You're bigger-framed.

Your dad could lift more so you can lift more. Your mom hit harder groundstrokes, so you can hit harder groundstrokes. You may even know more. And that's why you're better.

But that's not why you win.

That's not how you win.

You win because you're better at thinking about what you do.

You win because you understand the questions the game asks you to answer.

You win because you see opportunities no one else sees.

You win because you want it more.

Moneyball taught us what most people don't see.

And it's not all about the numbers.

Not really.

Not at all.

It's about seeing the right things clearly.

In baseball, it's all about on-base percentage.

You hit the ball on the equator. Great. I don't care.

You make the ball pop over the wall. Awesome. I don't care.

Your batting average rocks. Great. I don't care.

Your ERA is record-setting. Congratulations on the Cy Young. I don't care.

You get on-base 20% more often than the next guy. Sign 'im up.

Why???

Because the numbers say so.

Maybe. But that's not the whole story.

So why???

Because that is how you measure the players who hate to lose versus the players who love to win.

And that is all the difference.

But what is the on-base percentage in reality?

Players who love the winning feeling swing for the cheap seats.

Players who hate to lose get on base.

Any way they can.

Why?

Because players on base score.

Why do they care?

Because scoring wins. And winning is not losing.

And losing stinks.

Stars are stars.

We love them.

We sometimes worship them.

But stars are not what win ballgames. Races. Matches.

Stars may bring the fans out.

But players get on base.

And base hits win ballgames.

Why The Frame Matters

You can frame a painting. Frame a photograph. Place a great masterpiece on canvas inside one.

You can frame an argument. A concept. A proposal.

You can frame out a house. Frame a property.
Frame a master plan.

You can frame a composition, a setting for a still photograph, or a shot inside a motion picture.

You can be framed for something you didn't do. And you can frame Roger Rabbit.

And all of this framing can change the way you see the inherent truth of something.

How you frame the story of your brand makes all the difference.

It's not about the features and benefits.

As much as you've been taught it is…

As much as you want it to be…

It's not about the features and benefits.

And never has been.

It's not about how the features and benefits compare to your competition.

It's not about how you've revolutionized the sector… the industry… the world.

It's not about how much better you are or even that you're the best.

Even if you are.

Even if it is clear that you are.

There are many things it is not about.

It is partly about many more.

But it is only all about one.

One very clear thing.

It's all about how those things that make you different directly impact the people who matter to you.

It's all about how you frame the story to show them that you mean something important to them. As people. As human beings. Who live and work and move around in the world.

If they don't see how you make their lives better or easier or simpler, you won't matter to them at all.

Don't let them frame you.
Frame yourself into their lives.

Don't tell them.
Show them how it all fits together.

Part Two / Deciding Things

Why Ghosts Matter

Boo!

It can be frightening. Putting your thoughts out there.

Pen to paper.

Fingers to keys.

Ideas to work.

In front of people.

Who may judge. Certainly will judge. Which can be uncomfortable. Certainly will be uncomfortable.

But it's worth it. Because it's outside the comfort zone where the best things happen.

It can be trying. Trying to find the time.

You have the ideas. It's just the time that's elusive.

If you had the time, you'd put all of those unique and disruptive ideas out there into the ether to find their audience.

If you had the time, the world would hear what you have to say. Establish your reputation. Build your brand.

If you had the time, you'd write more.

If you had the time.

It can be difficult. Claiming the skills.

You hear it all the time. "Well, I'm no writer."

Or worse -- those who think all it takes is putting a verb between a subject and an object.

There's more to it, of course.

You know it.

You may even have the skill. But you recognize there are others who do it better. Others who do it with more panache. Or grace. Or compelling flair. And you want that. Maybe you need that. But you don't have the time or inclination to wrestle down the 10,000 hours to get it for yourself.

It can be challenging. Putting together a strategy for how to get your message across.

Every day.

To everyone.

Who matters.

You may know what you need.

Regular, original, brand stories.

Regular, original, educational material.

A social media voice.

A book.

A book, you say?

It can be overwhelming. Thinking about how to communicate your value in long-form.

A book? Yes a book.

Even a short, sales-tool book can be overwhelming to plan, structure, and execute.

But, do you want to know the secret?

There actually IS a secret to all of this.

You don't need to do it all yourself.

There are… out there in the atmosphere… floating in the ether… obliging ghosts not only willing, but eager to help you find your voice, guide your story, and write whatever it is you need for whatever purpose you envision.

All kinds of ghosts. With all kinds of ethereal skills.

The good ones will inspire and challenge you. They will help make your ideas better. They will enable others to see what you see.

Get one.

Get somebody who gets you.

Get somebody who listens to you.

Get somebody who feels your story the deep way you do.

Get somebody who can hear what you say, understand what you're trying to accomplish, listen to what it means, and convert it all into something that means something to the people who mean most.

Look for the ghosts.

We're out there.

Just say Boo!

Part Three
WRITING THINGS

Why Writing Matters

Good writing is a contact sport.

Hit 'em where it hurts.

Or where it matters most.

And it lets you control the action. And how they remember you.

Hit 'em hard enough to remember it forever.

So hard their ancestors feel it.

Like Tyson taking his first title in the second round.

Or UCLA undefeated in '64... and '67... and '72... and '73.

Or Annika carding 59.

Sometimes it's the dominance that earns a single name that lasts for generations.

Wilt.

Bannister.

Secretariat.

Sometimes, it's the anticipation that stands up a legend.

The greatest punch never thrown.

Do you believe in miracles?

The Giants win the pennant! The Giants win the pennant!

Good writing sticks with you like that.

And sometimes it's the surprise that satisfies.

The Called Shot in '32.

The Catch in '54.

The Immaculate Reception in '72.

It turns from something somebody said once into something you repeat over and over and over.

Something you direct others to do.

When you do it right.

Sometimes by accident. Sometimes just something in the moment. But it comes from the preparation. And the hard work. And that's what summons the right place at the right time out of the mist.

Take the time to hit 'em where it hurts. Or where it means most. Take the care to make them feel it.

That's what good writing is.

You feel it in your bones.

Your fists hurt.

You sweat.

You cry.

You bleed.

And if you do it right…

Your heart beats out of your chest.

And it takes your breath away.

Why Your Words Matter

I sat down to write you a short letter.

But I didn't have time.

So I wrote a long one instead.

Why does it take so long to write briefly?

Because it's harder than we all think.

Every time.

No matter how easy it was in our memory.

Because #wordsmatter

It takes time to write the right ones.

Into a thing that is meant to do something bigger. Something meaningful. Something important.

Sometimes you write something. And other times you wright something. And you always try to make it right.

It takes time to understand what you mean.

Because #wordsmatter

What you're trying to say… really.

What you truly mean.

Set aside the part where you consider how it's all going to be understood by someone else.

Someone you know.

Someone you don't.

Someone who you know has a background in what you're talking about.

Someone who doesn't.

Set aside the part where you care about how they see you.

What they think about you based on the words you choose.

What they can take away and tell other people about you. And what you do. And how it may be valuable to them. Or to others.

Set aside what they might misunderstand.

It takes consideration. Space. Silence. Preparation. Exploration. Inspiration.

Then it takes choices. Clear, purposeful choices. To cut. Change. Tighten. And polish.

One hundred and seventy-one thousand one hundred and forty-six words (171,146) in the English language alone.

Almost fifty thousand more declared obsolete.

There's a reason writers crumple up scribbled, exed-out, terrible, terrible pages and throw them across the room. Sometimes blank pages.
It's a ritual non-writers do not understand.

There is purpose in wastepaper. In making something by making a mess.

Because #wordsmatter

And it takes time to find the right ones.

And patience is a virtue.

The Romans used patientia meaning "to suffer."

And so we do when we try to write the right words.

And so we need to remember when we sit down again to write the right words.

Or ask someone else to.

Lying in wait for the right words to come. The words that work best.

I sat down to write you a short letter.

But I didn't have time.

So I wrote a long one instead.

And when I find the time, make the time, to write the right words…

It will be worth every moment.

Why Great Things Matter

What's the secret? To getting good at things? To improving things? To great things?

It's not glamorous.

There's no red carpet.

Or entourage to clear the path for you.

There's no stylist waiting to dress you or create an appearance for you to intrigue the world.

If you like those things, they can come later. Maybe.

It's not short-term satisfying like the fancy dessert or electrifying like the towering home run.

It doesn't come with a parade or a fireworks celebration.

It's quieter than all that. And the quiet things shout the loudest.

What's the secret? It's not really a secret.

But it's the thing that makes the difference.

Consistency.

Do it every day.

Find religion in it.

And that goes for anything you want to be good at in life.

You can find quotes from famous people about it all over the Internet.

"The harder I work, the luckier I get." Samuel Goldwyn.

"It takes 20 years to become an overnight success." Eddie Cantor.

Asked where did he find his secret? The golfing great, Ben Hogan said, "You dig it out of the dirt."

"Base hits win ballgames." Me.

In the content marketing game, Hubspot famously put out a study showing companies that publish 16 or more blog posts per month get 3.5 and 4.5 times more traffic than companies that post less than four items per month.

That's 3.5 for B2B and 4.5 for B2C, respectively.

They also showed 75% of their blog views and 90% of blog leads pointed to their posts published in the past. Sometimes long past.

So the good old stuff is sticky. It's valuable.

If you're making it, keep making it. If you're not, start. Start answering their questions. Before they ask them.

If you miss a day, get back to it the next day.

If you miss a week, get back into it next week.

If you miss a month… well, let's not miss a month.

If you can't do it, think about hiring someone who can. Because if you're doing nothing, you're falling behind.

Plan your plan.

Strategize your strategy.

Get your steps identified, written down, assigned, and plotted out for execution.

Then sit your hind quarters down in your chair and get it done.

Do the work.

Click the pen. Fire up the keyboard. Start typing and don't stop until it's done for the day.

Do the work. Again. Every day.

There is no secret.

It's just about getting the job done.

Every day.

Every day.

Every day.

Why Stories Matter

They call them stories for a reason.

The best magazine and newspaper articles all tell a tale; take you on a journey. It's a particular path from beginning-to-middle-to-end that humans inherently understand and respond to.

It's what makes them great.

And memorable.

And shareable.

The best bedtime stories begin with Once Upon a Time...

They introduce you to a main character on a journey. With a challenge. A purpose.

They make you sympathize with how the character overcomes each obstacle along the way. Happily Ever After.

Great business stories... Great Brand Stories... ALL do the same.

Great content tells a story. And takes you on a journey.

Great feature stories, speeches, presentations, ads, videos, movies, and elevator pitch stories... ALL of them.

Think about what content has moved you, yourself, to act. I'll bet it was a story and how that related to you, personally, that drove you to take the next step.

The best posts, emails, web content, articles, featurettes, all of them keep their readers engaged in a human way.

And humans LOVE stories. Telling them. Listening to them.
Sharing them with other people. It's the secret key to great communication.

Why Listening Matters

Read it one more time. Before.

Out loud.

I know you don't want to. Maybe you think you don't have to. But do it anyway.

Out loud.

Listen to your words. How they sound coming out into the air. How they feel in your mouth. What they taste like.

How they fill up your ears leaving room where it matters most.

Change it where it needs it.

Make it better. Smoother. Cleaner. Clearer.

Listen to the quiet places especially.

They make the loudest noise.

Then read it one more time. Before.

Maybe to someone else. Someone whose opinion matters to you.

Don't get angry about how they respond.

They are different than you. That's why you're sharing it with them in the first place.

It has rules. What we do.

Hear when they need to be ignored.

It has magic, sometimes, too.

And most people never, ever, see where the rabbit comes from.

Fix the punctuation. Put the i's and e's where they belong.
And in the right order.

But never forget there's music in what you've made. There's art in it.
And craft.

It's heard as much as it's read. What we do.

Maybe more.

And that is what's important.

Read it one more time. Before.

Then send it out into the world to sing its song.

Why Moments Matter

"People don't read anymore," they say.

They say it as if they're experts. But they're not.

As if they know. But they don't.

Not really.

It is true attention spans have waned over time. Twelve to eight and a quarter seconds. They say.

And it's more difficult to get them to spend time with what you have to say.

To capture, captivate, pique, and provoke.

But to say it as a blanket statement without even wanting to understand it… is…

Easy. Oversimplified.

Less than.

Lazy.

Ludicrous.

"People don't read anymore," they say.

I don't find that to be true. At all.

It's not as simple as that.

And I pay attention to it.

People don't read.

Much.

Until they want to.

Then they want to read everything.

They spend less time deciding.

There's so much content spinning around the globe right now.

2.5 quintillion bytes. Every day.

And they - that's the readers - choose to filter faster.

To find what matters to them.

Not just relevant, but significant.

The rest is chaff.

We need to write the way they read.

The best of us have always done.

People don't read.

Much.

Until they want to.

Then they want to read everything.

Why Brevity Matters

Brevity is the soul of wit, so says Polonius.

But also the soul of a great story, says I.

This is important because…

Your great product is only one part of how customers, clients, and members of your audience make their decisions.

The other, more important part, is how quickly they understand what you bring to them. That's when they choose.

Years ago, they say, Hemingway was sitting on a stool at the famed Algonquin Hotel Bar.

Surrounded by a collection of writers and other wits.

Eventually, a challenge was thrown down to the master of the short sentence.

How many words - more specifically - how few… does it take to create a complete story?

Beginning. Middle. End.

Six. Returned the old newsman.

A sawbuck made the stakes, tossed gauntlet-like onto the damp surface of the bar.

Papa took a pen from the pocket of one of his compatriots and jotted down the following on the back of a bar napkin and picked up his winnings.

FOR SALE. BABY SHOES. NEVER WORN.

Complete and perfect. A simple, evocative story of only six words with a beginning, a middle, and an end.

No matter that it's more than likely Hemingway had nothing to do with it.

A total fabrication.

But it sounds like Hemingway. It feels like Hemingway. Anchored in the truth of his economic prose and the known chip on his shoulder, it's believable that it could be Hemingway.

So it is.

The audaciousness and authenticity of the story leads us to not care if it is or if it is not.

We know immediately what the story is about and what it means.
And we love it. Because it's too good not to be true.

Mark Twain told us to never let the truth get in the way of a good story.

Or maybe he didn't.

That's another story.

Why Bangs Matter

The Exclamation Point. Sometimes called the exclamation mark.

Without doubt, the most childish of all punctuation.

We learn its use as children because we haven't yet the vocabulary to communicate properly without it.

It shows excitement. It transcends passion. Unveils anger, love, joy, frustration, and yet, it really doesn't do anything at all. A line and a dot.

In the newsroom, it's a "BANG."

"Put a BANG on that subhed!" Mainly because we're on deadline and haven't the few moments required for a thoughtful rewrite before a troop of union pressmen go on time and a half.

It's a terrible crutch that should be expunged from the language forever. We should aspire to greater.

J. J. Hagen, OSA. My professor and Augustinian literary confessor used to say it was a "theeere, now!" With a whiny finger-strike-swipe on the "theeere…"

We lean on it just because we have not time or imagination or proper superlative to use. And the longer we drift into digital doldrum, the fewer characters we're allowed to use.

Words suck up too many of our precious posts.

Just spell it shorter! When it goes viral, no one will care.

It's grammatical guvna (gówno – Polish for sh*t).

The bang makes us believe we've communicated with gusto when actually we've only shown ourselves weak.

A failed sentence. A weak expression in bold type.

Better to fail on the merit of an idea. Communicate with authenticity. The bang is a cheat. Fear not the fail.

"Ever tried. Ever failed. No matter. Try again. Fail again. Fail better." Samuel Beckett once said.

Use the words God and your teachers gave you. If you don't have enough, pull the big red-covered book down off the top shelf and put it to work.

Bang not, lest ye yourself be banged. And not in the good way.

We need to write well. With real words. And not let the punctuation carry us away.

The bang is nothing but a bang.

!!! end !!!

Why The Name Matters

Where is my badge? You'll never find it.

Naming things is hard.

Actually, naming things is easy. Naming things right is hard.

But sometimes, it's Kismet.

Sometimes, it's just silly.

The data is a little sketchy on the idea. Some people say the name of a brand matters deeply. Others say the value of the brand lifts the name and, therefore, makes it powerful.

There's little doubt, however, that when you make something, invent something, create something, there's an itch inside your mind and heart that compels you to really get the name right.

You want it to look right. Sound right. Feel right in your mouth.

You can always give it your name. The name of the founder.
You see these eponymous brand names everywhere. Ralph Lauren.
Martha Stewart. Lord & Taylor. Macy's.

The meaning of these names grows through the interaction their customers have with them over time.

But what about naming something original? Something that didn't exist before.

You want other people to remember you. To share it widely and feel strongly about it.

It's a little bit writing exercise - but it's not. It's an exercise of invention – sometimes. But it's more than that. When you nail it, it can seem like a lightning strike of inspiration. Poetry that you channel out of the ether.

And the people have no idea how hard it was.

Things get named for a reason.

And the right name can be powerful.

Sometimes the reason is obvious. It's named for what it does. Or what it looks like. The color. The sound. The shape. Or where it comes from.

New York Life. Arizona Iced Tea. Filene's Basement.

Sometimes the reason is about where, when, or how it's made. Twentieth design out of the shop, The Model T Ford.

And it can change. Once the people saw it, they called it The Tin Lizzie.

Sometimes, it's the address. Saks Fifth Avenue. Studio 54.

Sometimes, it's clever. Nike. Cadillac. Starbucks.

Sometimes a name can be so clever it sinks itself under it's own weight.

Meta.

And sometimes… it comes out of a story so silly as to defy explanation.

In 1968, George Harrison was scribbling down notes for a new song he was working on with his friend, Eric Clapton.

When Clapton stole a peek across the table, he said Badge!
That's a good title!

The only problem. Clapton misread Harrison's handwriting of the word "bridge" upside down noting the bridge of the song.

But the title stuck. And the recurring chorus, "where is my badge?" was born and recorded on Cream's last album.

One of the most memorable songs immortalized by one of the most beloved guitarists and songwriters was titled completely by accident.

Sometimes the name of a thing is all about a feeling. And that's how it sticks.

And has nothing to do whatever with what it does, or why it's valuable, or how it's different, or how it might make the world a better place.

Sometimes it's just satisfying to sing "where is my badge?"

Why The Hard Things Matter

Writing is in everything.

And it isn't easy.

This for those of you who insist on saying things like, "I'm not a writer."

You are. Everything you create involves writing it.

Telling it.

Pushing it on to others so that they can tell others.

You come up with the concept. The idea.

You work out the story, that is, what you want to tell other people about what you're thinking. Then you polish it until it's ready.

Sometimes past the time when it's ready.

Sometimes you question whether it's overcooked.

Then you loose it upon the world hoping to have an impact.

Presuming you'll have an impact.

It is hard.

It is hard to be competent.

It is hard to be good.

It is even harder to be great.

It is near impossible to be inspired.

And yet, they think because you have a happy talent for it, it must be, somehow, easier for you.

It is not.

And it never will be.

When you start a new thing, you start from scratch. Every time.

Being understood takes time. And effort. And forethought. And a nimble facility with language.

Being understood sometimes takes luck. And timing. And patience.

And patience comes from the Latin meaning to suffer.

Which is why it takes time. And effort. To think up and write something of value.

And it is the reason writers should hold the reins of power at creative agencies.

They always used to.

It wasn't until the dawn of TV that the designers started climbing to the top.

WRITING IS HARD.

You feel the pain and sweat and effort in it.

And only when it is done, do you see the path forward.

But there are those who can't see it.

They think writing is easy. For the writers.

It is not.

It is a kind of torture.

But when it is done.

When it is good.

There is sometimes satisfaction.

Sometimes there is joy in having written.

One more.
WITH FEELING.

Why Your Word Work Matters

Take 'em to ♡🖤♡ and you'll write better, stronger, more effective content, too.

1. Have a voice.
Every author has one. Every brand does too. Establish yours. And be consistent across all communications.

2. Take a position.
It's called the point of attack. Attitude. Have one. And tell them why it's important.

3. Keep it tight.
Short, crisp sentences and paragraphs make a difference.
Write the way they read.

4. Don't believe your own press.
Sure, people say you're great. And that may buy you an extra second of attention, but readers are impatient and easily distracted. If you're not sure... go back and read #3 again.

5. Five seconds at a time.
They only give you about 5 seconds at a time. Look at your watch. Now. Count to 5. That's it. All you get. Really. Believe it.

6. Include links. Always.
So you're writing. For people. To learn something. Include links. Don't ask. Just do it. "But I'm writing for print," you say... Include links there, too. If they're simple and easy to remember.

7. If you're funny, be funny.
Make them cry and they'll love you. Make them laugh and they'll remember you. Then they'll tell their friends.

8. But not too funny.
Be careful, though. Not everyone thinks the same things are funny. And you may not be as funny as you think you are. Learn what your audience likes and laughs at. Then do more of that.

9. Always be ACTIVE.
No. Don't get up to do jumping jacks. Make your writing active. If you want your readers to do something. Tell them. Never expect that they're just going to get it. Tell them.

10. Embrace the fundamentals.
If you're gifted, go back and read #9 again until your call to action makes sense. Don't take shortcuts. Master the basics. Then go back and remind yourself of the basics again. If you're asking yourself right now if you're gifted. You're not. Go back and read #9 again. And then #3, again, too.

11. In Brief... Be BRIEF.

The Lord's Prayer - 66 words.

The 10 Commandments - 179 words.

The Gettysburg address - 286 words.

The Declaration of Independence - 1,458 words.

US federal regulations on the sale of cabbage - 26,911 words.

Which one do you remember best?

That's All She Wrote.

That's it.

That's all there is.

I've called it volume one because I believe there's more to come.

And that's what this little book is about in the end, belief.

What you believe about things.

How to do things.

Why we do things.

How other people should know more about how we do things.

Whether I'm right or wrong. Or something in between.

Take this one bit of advice.

Think about things.

More.

More often.

More deeply.

And put that to work.

Be honest. Be authentic. Think about everything in you that makes you, and the way you do things, different than everyone else.

And that makes all the difference.

Acknowledgements

As I said in the introduction, I never set out to write this book. It evolved from a series of short pieces I wrote that I thought would help people understand what each other are trying to communicate to each other every day. That said, it is now a book that I hope will help achieve that end for some of my readers and it would not have seen the light of day without the help and inspiration from my family, Heather and Aiden who put up with my constant requests to read something more, even if just a few words have been changed. My stuff would not be readable without their help. Inspiration from my way of thinking comes from almost every job I've ever had, but most recently, friends and colleagues I trusted to show this to before releasing it were invaluable. To Rocket for everything and a spectacular cover and book design, Jordan in ME, Dave who is genuinely one of the funniest humans I ever met, Qaadirah in Atlanta, Jim & Sarah in CA, Brett in MI, Peggy in NJ, and Carl in the UK. Thank you for your input, your insight, your corrections, and all of those times you told me these thoughts spoke to you in one way or another. Thank you Katy for your sharp eyes and even sharper pencil. I've called it "vol. 1" believing that even if it's just you great and wonderful people, there will be a "vol. 2."

About The Author

Born and raised in the Garden State, Lyle Smith has a substantial northeastern small state chip on his shoulder about most things, but loves everybody anyway. He's been a daily newspaper reporter, editor, in-house marketing executive, agency creative director, and for more than the past decade, chief of his own consulting brand story agency called Nymblesmith where he helps small to mid-sized businesses get their stories straight so their customers recognize the depth of their value. He's been a runner, a caddie, a grave-digger and he believes if everyone worked in a service job at some point in their careers, the world would be a much happier and more agreeable place. He currently resides in Boulder Valley, CO, drawing daily inspiration from his wife, Heather, a leading acupuncturist and fertility specialist in her field and his son, Aiden, a truly old soul who forever gives him a new angle from which to view the world.

www.ingramcontent.com/pod-product-compliance
Lightning Source LLC
Chambersburg PA
CBHW070719130626
46553CB00005B/2064

9 7 9 8 9 8 9 2 6 5 9 0 9